ARTIFICIAL INTELLIGENCE AND SERVERLESS MACHINE LEARNING FOR BEGINNERS

A Step-by-Step Guide to Building Intelligent Applications with Cloud-Based Machine Learning Services

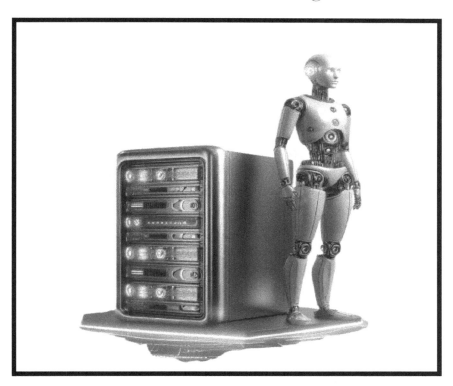

Saul E. Sanchez

DISCLAIMER

The information contained within this book is intended for general knowledge and informational purposes only. It is not a substitute for professional advice. While all efforts have been made to ensure accuracy, the author(s) and publisher cannot guarantee the completeness or accuracy of the information presented.

The author(s) and publisher assume no responsibility for any errors, omissions, or damages arising from the use of the information contained herein. Readers are encouraged to verify information with additional sources and consult with professionals as needed.

The inclusion of any third-party content or links does not constitute an endorsement or recommendation by the author(s) or publisher.

About the Author

Saul E. Sanchez is a seasoned data scientist and software engineer with a passion for leveraging data to drive innovation. With a strong foundation in statistical modeling, machine learning, and programming languages like Python, Saul Sanchez has a proven track record of delivering impactful data-driven solutions.

Saul Sanchez excels in data analysis, feature engineering, model building, and deployment. Their expertise spans a wide range of techniques, including supervised and unsupervised learning, deep learning, and natural language processing. They are proficient in using tools like TensorFlow, PyTorch, Scikit-learn, and Pandas to extract valuable insights from complex datasets.

Beyond technical skills, Saul Sanchez is dedicated to ethical AI and data privacy. They strive to develop models that are fair, transparent, and responsible.

TABLE OF CONTENTS

PART I: FOUNDATIONS OF ARTIFICIAL INTELLIGENCE AND MACHINE LEARNING

Chapter 1: Introduction to Artificial Intelligence and Machine Learning

What is Artificial Intelligence?

Artificial Intelligence (AI) is a branch of computer science that aims to create intelligent agents, which are systems that can reason, learn, and act autonomously. It involves developing algorithms and techniques that enable machines to mimic human intelligence.

Key Components of AI:

1. Machine Learning: A subset of AI that focuses on algorithms that learn patterns from data and make predictions or decisions.
- Supervised Learning: Training a model on labeled data to make predictions or classifications.
- Unsupervised Learning: Finding patterns in unlabeled data without explicit guidance.
- Reinforcement Learning: Learning through trial and error, where an agent learns to make decisions based on rewards and penalties.

2. Natural Language Processing (NLP): The ability of computers to understand, interpret, and generate human language.
- Text Analysis: Extracting meaning and sentiment from text data.
- Machine Translation: Translating text from one language to another.
- Text Generation: Creating human-quality text, such as articles or poetry.

3. Computer Vision: Enabling computers to interpret and understand visual information from the world.
- Image Recognition: Identifying objects and scenes in images.
- Object Detection: Locating and classifying objects within an image.
- Image Segmentation: Dividing an image into meaningful regions.

4. Robotics: Designing and building robots that can perform tasks autonomously or with human guidance.

- Industrial Robotics: Automation of manufacturing processes.
- Service Robotics: Robots for tasks like cleaning, delivery, and healthcare.

Real-world Applications of AI:
- Healthcare: Medical diagnosis, drug discovery, and personalized medicine.
- Finance: Fraud detection, algorithmic trading, and risk assessment.
- Autonomous Vehicles: Self-driving cars and drones.
- Customer Service: Chatbots and virtual assistants.
- Recommendation Systems: Personalized product recommendations.

AI has the potential to revolutionize various industries and improve our lives in countless ways. it is important to consider the ethical implications and societal impact of AI, such as job displacement and bias in algorithms.

A Brief History of AI

The concept of artificial intelligence has been around for centuries, but its modern form began to take shape in the mid-20th century. Here's a brief overview of key milestones in AI's history:

Early AI (1950s-1970s)

- Alan Turing's Turing Test: In 1950, Turing proposed a test to determine whether a machine could exhibit intelligent behavior equivalent to, or indistinguishable from, that of a human.
- Early AI Programs: Researchers developed early AI programs that could solve simple problems like playing checkers and proving mathematical theorems.

AI Winter (1970s-1980s)

- Limitations of Early AI: The limitations of early AI techniques and the lack of computational power led to a period of disillusionment known as the "AI winter."

AI Renaissance (1980s-Present)
- Expert Systems: AI systems designed to mimic the decision-making ability of human experts.
- Machine Learning Advancements: Significant advancements in machine learning algorithms, particularly neural networks, led to breakthroughs in various AI applications.
- Big Data and Cloud Computing: The availability of massive amounts of data and powerful computing resources fueled the growth of AI.
- Deep Learning Revolution: Deep learning, a subset of machine learning, has enabled significant advancements in fields like computer vision, natural language processing, and speech recognition.
- AI in Everyday Life: AI is now integrated into many aspects of our lives, from smartphones to autonomous vehicles.

Types of AI

Artificial Intelligence can be categorized into three main types:

1. Narrow AI (Weak AI)
Definition: Narrow AI is designed to perform a specific task.
Examples:
- Image recognition: Identifying objects in images.
- Speech recognition: Converting spoken language into text.
- Recommendation systems: Suggesting products or content based on user preferences.
- Self-driving cars: Navigating roads and making driving decisions.

2. General AI (Strong AI)
Definition: General AI refers to AI that possesses human-level intelligence and can understand, learn, and apply knowledge across a wide range of tasks.

- Current Status: While there have been significant advancements in AI, true general AI is still hypothetical.

3. Superintelligence

Definition: Superintelligence surpasses human intelligence and capabilities in every aspect, including creativity, problem-solving, and social skills.
- Potential Implications: The development of superintelligence raises ethical concerns and questions about its potential impact on humanity.

What is Machine Learning?

Machine Learning is a subset of artificial intelligence that focuses on algorithms that learn patterns from data and make predictions or decisions without explicit programming. It enables systems to improve their performance over time by learning from experience.

Key Concepts in Machine Learning:
- Model: A mathematical representation of a real-world phenomenon.
- Training Data: A dataset used to train the model.
- Features: The input variables used to train the model.
- Labels: The output variable(s) that the model predicts.
- Algorithm: The procedure used to learn patterns from the training data.
- Prediction: The output generated by the model for new, unseen data.

Types of Machine Learning:
1. Supervised Learning:
Training data is labeled with the correct output.
The model learns to map inputs to outputs.
Examples:
- Regression: Predicting a continuous numerical value (e.g., house prices).
- Classification: Categorizing data into discrete classes (e.g., spam detection).

2. Unsupervised Learning:
Training data is unlabeled.
The model discovers hidden patterns and structures in the data.

Examples:
- Clustering: Grouping similar data points together.
- Dimensionality Reduction: Reducing the number of features in a dataset.

3. Reinforcement Learning:
An agent learns to make decisions by interacting with an environment.
The agent receives rewards or penalties based on its actions.
Examples:
- Game playing (e.g., AlphaGo)
- Robotics

Types of Machine Learning

1. Supervised Learning
In supervised learning, the algorithm is trained on a dataset where the correct output (label) is provided for each input. The goal is to learn a mapping function that can accurately predict the output for new, unseen input data.
Key techniques:
- Regression: Predicting a continuous numerical value (e.g., house prices, stock prices).
- Classification: Categorizing data into discrete classes (e.g., spam detection, image classification).

2. Unsupervised Learning
In unsupervised learning, the algorithm is trained on unlabeled data. The goal is to discover hidden patterns and structures within the data.

Key techniques:
- Clustering: Grouping similar data points together.
- Dimensionality Reduction: Reducing the number of features in a dataset.
- Anomaly Detection: Identifying unusual data points that deviate from the norm.

3. Reinforcement Learning

In reinforcement learning, an agent learns to make decisions by interacting with an environment. The agent receives rewards or penalties based on its actions and learns to maximize cumulative reward over time.

Key concepts:
- Agent: The decision-making entity.
- Environment: The external world the agent interacts with.
- State: The current situation or configuration of the environment.
- Action: The choice made by the agent.
- Reward: The feedback received by the agent for its action.

Real-world applications:
Game playing: Training AI agents to play games like chess, Go, and video games.
Robotics: Controlling robots to perform tasks in complex environments.
Autonomous vehicles: Making decisions about steering, acceleration, and braking.

Understanding these different types of machine learning, can harness its power to solve complex problems and drive innovation.

Chapter 2: Essential Mathematical Concepts

Machine learning heavily relies on mathematical concepts to understand and process data. Here are some fundamental mathematical concepts that are essential for anyone interested in machine learning:

Linear Algebra
Linear algebra is the branch of mathematics concerned with the study of vectors, matrices, and linear transformations.

- Vectors: A vector is a sequence of numbers arranged in a column or row.
- Matrices: A matrix is a rectangular array of numbers arranged in rows and columns.
- Matrix Operations:
  - Matrix addition and subtraction
  - Matrix multiplication
  - Matrix inversion
  - Transposition
  - Determinant
  - Eigenvalues and eigenvectors

Calculus
Calculus is the branch of mathematics concerned with rates of change and accumulation of quantities.

- Derivatives: The derivative measures the rate of change of a function at a specific point.
- Gradients: The gradient is a vector that points in the direction of steepest ascent of a function.
- Partial Derivatives: A partial derivative measures the rate of change of a function with respect to one variable, while holding other variables constant.

Probability and Statistics

Probability and statistics are the branches of mathematics concerned with uncertainty and data analysis.

- Probability: The study of chance and randomness.
- Probability Distributions: Functions that describe the likelihood of different outcomes.
- Statistical Inference: Drawing conclusions about a population based on a sample.
- Hypothesis Testing: Making decisions about population parameters based on sample data.

These mathematical concepts are fundamental to understanding and implementing machine learning algorithms. You can gain a deeper understanding of how machine learning models work and how to build effective models.

Linear Algebra

Vectors

A vector is a fundamental concept in linear algebra, representing a quantity that has both magnitude and direction. It can be visualized as an arrow pointing from an origin to a specific point in space.

Example: A 2D vector can represent a point in a plane:

$v = [2, 3]$

Here, the vector `v` has a magnitude of `$sqrt(2^2 + 3^2) = sqrt(13)$` and points in the direction specified by the coordinates **(2, 3).**

Matrices

A matrix is a rectangular array of numbers arranged in rows and columns. Matrices are used to represent linear transformations, systems of equations, and data.

Example: A 2x3 matrix:
```
A = [[1, 2, 3],
     [4, 5, 6]]
```

Matrix Operations

1. Matrix Addition and Subtraction: Two matrices of the same dimensions can be added or subtracted element-wise.

2. Matrix Multiplication: The product of two matrices is defined only if the number of columns in the first matrix equals the number of rows in the second matrix.

The resulting matrix has dimensions equal to the number of rows of the first matrix and the number of columns of the second matrix.

3. Matrix Transposition: The transpose of a matrix is obtained by interchanging its rows and columns.

4. Matrix Inversion: The inverse of a square matrix A, denoted as A^{-1}, is a matrix such that $A * A^{-1} = I$, where I is the identity matrix.

5. Determinant: The determinant of a square matrix is a scalar value that characterizes the matrix. It is used to solve systems of linear equations and find eigenvalues and eigenvectors.

6. Eigenvalues and Eigenvectors: An eigenvector of a square matrix A is a non zero vector v such that $Av = \lambda v$, where λ is a scalar called the eigenvalue.

These linear algebra concepts are essential for understanding machine learning algorithms, as they are used to represent data, perform calculations, and optimize models.

Calculus: Derivatives and Gradients

Calculus is a branch of mathematics that deals with rates of change and accumulation of quantities. In machine learning, calculus is fundamental for optimization techniques, such as gradient descent, which is used to minimize the error of a model.

Derivatives

A derivative measures the rate of change of a function at a specific point. It represents the slope of the tangent line to the function's graph at that point.

Notation:
Leibniz notation: `dy/dx`
Lagrange notation: `f'(x)`

Example

Consider the function `f(x) = x^2`. The derivative of `f(x)` with respect to `x` is `f'(x) = 2x`. This means that the slope of the tangent line to the graph of `f(x)` at any point `x` is `2x`.

Gradients

A gradient is a vector that points in the direction of the steepest increase of a function. In the context of multivariable functions, the gradient is a vector of partial derivatives.

Example:

Consider the function `f(x, y) = x^2 + y^2`. The gradient of `f(x, y)` is given by:

```
```

$$\nabla f(x, y) = [\partial f/\partial x, \partial f/\partial y] = [2x, 2y]$$
```
```

Gradient Descent is an optimization algorithm that iteratively moves in the direction of the negative gradient to find the minimum of a function. This is widely used in machine learning to minimize the error of a model.

Probability and Statistics

Probability and statistics are essential tools for understanding uncertainty and making data-driven decisions. They play a crucial role in machine learning, particularly in areas like probabilistic modeling, Bayesian inference, and statistical hypothesis testing.

Probability

Probability theory deals with the study of random events and their likelihood of occurrence. Key concepts include:

- Random Variable: A variable whose value is a numerical outcome of a random phenomenon.
- Probability Distribution: A function that describes the likelihood of different outcomes of a random variable.
- Probability Density Function (PDF): A function that describes the probability distribution of a continuous random variable.
- Probability Mass Function (PMF): A function that describes the probability distribution of a discrete random variable.

Bayes' Theorem

Bayes' theorem is a fundamental rule of probability that allows us to update our beliefs about a hypothesis as new evidence becomes available. It is expressed as:

```
P(A|B) = P(B|A) * P(A) / P(B)
```

Where:
- P(A|B): The probability of A given B
- P(B|A): The probability of B given A

- P(A): The prior probability of A
- P(B): The prior probability of B

Hypothesis Testing
Hypothesis testing is a statistical method used to determine whether a hypothesis about a population parameter is true or false. It involves setting up a null hypothesis (H_0) and an alternative hypothesis (H_1) and then collecting data to test these hypotheses.

Key concepts:
- Null Hypothesis (H_0): A statement that there is no effect or difference.
- Alternative Hypothesis (H_1): A statement that contradicts the null hypothesis.
- Test Statistic: A numerical value calculated from sample data to test the hypothesis.
- P-value: The probability of observing a test statistic as extreme or more extreme than the one calculated, assuming the null hypothesis is true.
- Significance Level (α): The threshold for rejecting the null hypothesis.

These fundamental concepts can be applied to various machine learning tasks, such as building probabilistic models, making Bayesian inferences, and evaluating the significance of experimental results.

Chapter 3: Introduction to Python Programming

Python is a versatile and powerful programming language that has become increasingly popular for data science and machine learning. Its simplicity and readability make it an excellent choice for beginners and experienced programmers alike.

Setting Up the Python Environment

1. Download and Install Python:

- Visit the official Python website: [https://www.python.org/downloads/](https://www.google.com/url?sa=E&source=gmail&q=https://www.python.org/downloads/)
- Download the latest Python version: Choose the appropriate installer for your operating system (Windows, macOS, or Linux).
- Follow the installation instructions: Typically, you'll be guided through a straightforward installation process.

2. Choose an IDE or Text Editor:

An Integrated Development Environment (IDE) or a text editor provides a user-friendly interface for writing and running Python code. Here are some popular options:

IDE:
- PyCharm: A powerful IDE with features like code completion, debugging, and version control.
- Visual Studio Code: A versatile code editor that can be customized with various extensions for Python development.

Text Editor:
- Sublime Text: A lightweight and highly customizable text editor.
- Notepad++: A free source code editor, especially popular on Windows.

3. Install Essential Libraries:

To work with data science and machine learning, you'll need to install several essential Python libraries. The most common ones include:

- NumPy: For numerical computations and array operations.
- Pandas: For data analysis and manipulation.
- Matplotlib: For creating visualizations.
- Scikit-learn: For machine learning algorithms.
- TensorFlow and PyTorch: For deep learning.
- Using `pip` to Install Libraries:`pip` is a package installer for Python. You can use it to install libraries from the Python Package Index (PyPI).

```bash
pip install numpy pandas matplotlib scikit-learn tensorflow pytorch
```

- Using Anaconda or Miniconda: If you've installed Anaconda or Miniconda, you can use the `conda` package manager to install libraries:

```bash
conda install -c conda-forge numpy pandas matplotlib scikit-learn tensorflow pytorch
```

4. Verify the Installation:

Open your chosen IDE or text editor and create a new Python file. Write a simple Python script to print "Hello, World\!":

```python
print("Hello, World!")
```

Run the script. If you see the output "Hello, World\!" in the console, your Python environment is set up correctly.

With a well-configured Python environment, you're ready to embark on your data science and machine learning journey.

Basic Python Syntax and Data Structures

Basic Syntax

Indentation:
- Python uses indentation to define code blocks.
- It's crucial to maintain consistent indentation (usually 4 spaces) within a code block.

```python
if 5 > 2:
    print("Five is greater than two!")
```

Comments:
- Use `#` to add comments to your code. Comments are ignored by the interpreter.

```python
# This is a comment
print("Hello, world!")
```

Variables:
- Declare variables without specifying a data type.
- Use the assignment operator `=` to assign values.

```python
x = 5  # Integer
y = 3.14  # Float
name = "Alice"  # String
```

Operators:

- Arithmetic operators: `+`, `-`, `*`, `/`, `//` (floor division), `%` (modulo), `**` (exponentiation)
- Comparison operators: `==`, `!=`, `<`, `>`, `<=`, `>=`
- Logical operators: `and`, `or`, `not`

Data Structures

Numbers:

- Integers: Whole numbers (e.g., 1, -10, 100)
- Floating-point numbers: Numbers with decimal points (e.g., 3.14, -2.5)

Strings:

- Sequences of characters enclosed in single or double quotes.
- Can be manipulated using various string methods (e.g., slicing, concatenation, formatting).

```python
name = "Alice"
greeting = "Hello, " + name + "!"
```

Lists:

- Ordered collections of items, mutable.
- Elements can be accessed and modified using indexing.

```python
fruits = ["apple", "banana", "cherry"]
print(fruits[1])  # Access the second element
```

Tuples:

- Ordered collections of items, immutable.
- Useful for representing fixed data.

```python
coordinates = (10, 20)
```

Sets:
- Unordered collections of unique items.
- Used for membership testing and eliminating duplicates.

```python
my_set = {1, 2, 3, 3}  # Duplicates are removed
```

Dictionaries:
- Key-value pairs.
- Keys must be unique and immutable.

```python
person = {"name": "Alice", "age": 30, "city": "New York"}
```

With these basic concepts, you can start writing Python code to solve various problems and build more complex applications.

NumPy and Pandas for Data Manipulation

NumPy and **Pandas** are two powerful Python libraries that are essential for data science and machine learning. They provide efficient tools for data manipulation, analysis, and visualization.

NumPy

NumPy, short for Numerical Python, is a library for numerical computations. It introduces the `ndarray` object, which is a multi-dimensional array optimized for numerical operations.

Key features of NumPy:

- Efficient array operations: Perform element-wise operations, matrix operations, and linear algebra.
- Array creation: Create arrays using various methods like `np.array`, `np.zeros`, `np.ones`, and `np.random.rand`.
- Array indexing and slicing: Access and manipulate array elements using indexing and slicing techniques.
- Universal functions: Apply functions element-wise to arrays.
- Linear algebra operations: Perform matrix multiplication, inversion, and eigenvalue decomposition.

Example:

```python
import numpy as np

# Create a NumPy array
arr = np.array([1, 2, 3, 4, 5])

# Perform array operations
print(arr * 2)  # Element-wise multiplication
print(np.mean(arr))  # Calculate the mean

# Create a 2D array
matrix = np.array([[1, 2], [3, 4]])

# Matrix multiplication
print(np.dot(matrix, matrix.T))
```

Pandas

Pandas is a library built on top of NumPy, providing high-performance data structures and data analysis tools. It introduces two primary data structures: `Series` and `DataFrame`.

Key features of Pandas:

- Series: A one-dimensional array-like object with labels.
- DataFrame: A two-dimensional labeled data structure with columns that can hold different data types.
- Data ingestion: Read data from various file formats (CSV, Excel, JSON, etc.).
- Data cleaning and preparation: Handle missing values, outliers, and inconsistent data.
- Data analysis: Perform statistical calculations, filtering, sorting, and grouping operations.
- Data visualization: Create visualizations using built-in plotting functions or external libraries like Matplotlib and Seaborn.

Example:

```python
import pandas as pd

# Create a DataFrame
data = {'Name': ['Alice', 'Bob', 'Charlie'],
    'Age': [25, 30, 28],
    'City': ['New York', 'Los Angeles', 'Chicago']}
df = pd.DataFrame(data)

# Display the DataFrame
print(df)

# Access specific columns and rows
print(df['Age'])
print(df.loc[1])

# Calculate summary statistics
print(df.describe())
```

By mastering NumPy and Pandas, you'll be able to efficiently manipulate and analyze large datasets, which is a crucial skill for data science and machine learning.

Matplotlib and Seaborn for Data Visualization

Matplotlib and **Seaborn** are powerful Python libraries used to create a wide range of visualizations. They allow you to explore and communicate data effectively.

Matplotlib

Matplotlib is a versatile library that provides a low-level interface for creating static, animated, and interactive visualizations. It offers a wide range of plot types, including:

- Line plots: Visualize trends and patterns over time.
- Scatter plots: Show relationships between two variables.
- Bar charts: Compare categorical data.
- Histograms: Visualize the distribution of numerical data.
- Box plots: Show the distribution of data, including quartiles and outliers.
- Pie charts: Display proportions of different categories.

Basic Example:

```python
import matplotlib.pyplot as plt
import numpy as np

x = np.linspace(0, 10, 100)
y = np.sin(x)

plt.plot(x, y)
plt.xlabel('x')
plt.ylabel('sin(x)')
plt.title('Sine Wave')
plt.show()
```

Seaborn

Seaborn is a high-level data visualization library built on top of Matplotlib. It provides a more attractive and informative visualization style, often requiring less code than Matplotlib.

Key features of Seaborn:
- Statistical visualizations: Create informative visualizations like pair plots, heatmaps, and cluster maps.
- Customizable styles: Easily customize the appearance of plots with different styles and color palettes.
- Seaborn-specific plot types: Offers specialized plot types like violin plots, catplots, and joint plots.

Basic Example:

```python
import seaborn as sns
import matplotlib.pyplot as plt
import pandas as pd

# Sample DataFrame
tips = sns.load_dataset("tips")

# Create a scatter plot
sns.scatterplot(x="total_bill", y="tip", hue="smoker", data=tips)
plt.show()
```

Combining the power of Matplotlib and Seaborn, you can create a wide range of visualizations to explore and communicate your data effectively.

PART II: SERVERLESS COMPUTING AND CLOUD PLATFORMS

Chapter 4: Understanding Serverless Computing

Serverless computing is a cloud computing execution model where the cloud provider automatically manages the allocation of machine resources required to run an application. This eliminates the need for developers to provision and manage servers, allowing them to focus on writing and deploying code.

Key Concepts in Serverless Computing

1. Function as a Service (FaaS):
- The core concept of serverless computing.
- Developers write small, independent functions that are triggered by events.
- The cloud provider automatically scales the infrastructure to handle the workload.

2. Event-Driven Architecture:
- Applications are designed around events and triggers.
- Events can be generated by various sources, such as API calls, database changes, or messages from other services.
- Functions are executed in response to these events.

3. Scalability and Elasticity:
- Serverless functions can automatically scale up or down based on the incoming workload.
- This ensures optimal resource utilization and cost-efficiency.

4. Pay-Per-Use Pricing:
- You only pay for the compute time consumed by your functions.
- This eliminates the need to pay for idle servers.

Benefits of Serverless Computing

- Reduced Operational Overhead: No need to manage servers, operating systems, or infrastructure.
- Faster Time to Market: Rapid deployment and scaling of applications.
- Improved Scalability: Automatic scaling to handle varying workloads.
- Cost-Efficiency: Pay-per-use pricing model.
- Higher Developer Productivity: Focus on writing code, not managing infrastructure.

Common Use Cases for Serverless Computing
- Real-time Data Processing: Analyze and process data streams in real-time.
- Web and Mobile Backends: Build scalable and efficient backends for web and mobile applications.
- IoT Applications: Process data from IoT devices and trigger actions.
- Microservices Architectures: Break down complex applications into smaller, independent services.

Popular Serverless Platforms
- AWS Lambda: A serverless computing platform provided by Amazon Web Services.
- Google Cloud Functions: A serverless computing platform provided by Google Cloud Platform.
- Azure Functions: A serverless computing platform provided by Microsoft Azure.

The Serverless Paradigm

The serverless paradigm represents a shift in how applications are built and deployed. It abstracts away the underlying infrastructure, allowing developers to focus on writing the core business logic without worrying about managing servers.

Key characteristics of the serverless paradigm:

Function-as-a-Service (FaaS):
- Applications are broken down into small, independent functions.

- Each function is triggered by an event, such as an HTTP request, a database change, or a message from a queue.
- The cloud provider automatically manages the execution environment, scaling resources up or down as needed.

Event-Driven Architecture:
- Applications are designed around events and triggers.
- Events can be generated by various sources, including user actions, system events, or data changes.
- Functions are invoked in response to these events, creating a loosely coupled and scalable architecture.

Pay-Per-Use Pricing:
- You only pay for the compute time consumed by your functions, making it a cost-effective solution for many applications.

Automatic Scaling:
- Serverless platforms automatically scale the number of instances to handle the workload, ensuring optimal performance and reliability.

Advantages of Serverless Computing:
- Reduced Operational Overhead: No need to manage servers, operating systems, or infrastructure.
- Faster Time to Market: Rapid deployment and scaling of applications.
- Improved Scalability: Automatic scaling to handle varying workloads.
- Cost-Efficiency: Pay-per-use pricing model.
- Higher Developer Productivity: Focus on writing code, not managing infrastructure.

Common Use Cases for Serverless Computing:
- Real-time Data Processing: Analyze and process data streams in real-time.
- Web and Mobile Backends: Build scalable and efficient backends for web and mobile applications.
- IoT Applications: Process data from IoT devices and trigger actions.
- Microservices Architectures: Break down complex applications into smaller, independent services.

Benefits of Serverless Computing

Serverless computing offers a number of advantages that can significantly improve the development and deployment of applications:

Reduced Operational Overhead
- No server management: Eliminates the need to manage server infrastructure, including provisioning, patching, and scaling.
- Simplified operations: Focus on application development and deployment, rather than infrastructure maintenance.

Faster Time to Market
- Rapid deployment: Quickly deploy and iterate on applications without the overhead of provisioning and configuring servers.
- Accelerated development: Developers can focus on writing code, leading to faster development cycles.

Improved Scalability
- Automatic scaling: Serverless platforms automatically scale resources up or down based on demand, ensuring optimal performance and cost-efficiency.
- Seamless handling of traffic spikes: Easily handle sudden increases in traffic without worrying about infrastructure limitations.

Cost-Efficiency
- Pay-per-use pricing: Pay only for the compute time consumed by your functions, reducing costs.
- Elimination of idle resources: Avoid paying for idle servers, as resources are allocated dynamically.

Higher Developer Productivity
- Focus on core business logic: Developers can concentrate on writing application code, rather than infrastructure concerns.
- Simplified development workflow: Streamlined development and deployment processes.

Serverless Functions and Event-Driven Architecture

Serverless Functions

Serverless functions are the building blocks of serverless computing. They are small, self-contained units of code that can be triggered by events. These functions are executed in a stateless manner, meaning they don't maintain any persistent state between invocations.

Key characteristics of serverless functions:

- Event-driven: Triggered by events, such as HTTP requests, database changes, or messages from other services.
- Stateless: Each function execution is independent and doesn't maintain state between invocations.
- Scalable: Automatically scaled to handle varying workloads.
- Pay-per-use: You only pay for the compute time consumed by your functions.

Event-Driven Architecture

Event-driven architecture (EDA) is a design pattern that relies on events to trigger actions. In a serverless context, events can trigger the execution of serverless functions.

Key components of EDA:

- Event Source: Generates events, such as user actions, system events, or data changes.
- Event Bus: A mechanism for distributing events to interested subscribers.
- Event Consumer: A function or service that processes the event and performs an action.

Benefits of Event-Driven Architecture:

- Decoupling: Components can be loosely coupled, making the system more flexible and resilient.
- Scalability: Events can be processed independently, allowing for easy scaling.
- Real-time Processing: Events can be processed as soon as they occur.

- Asynchronous Processing: Non-critical tasks can be processed asynchronously, improving performance.

Example:
Consider a simple e-commerce application. When a user places an order, an event is generated. This event can trigger multiple functions:

1. Order Processing Function: Processes the order and updates the inventory.
2. Email Notification Function: Sends a confirmation email to the user.
3. Analytics Function: Collects data for analytics and reporting.

By breaking down the application into smaller, independent functions, the system becomes more scalable, resilient, and easier to maintain.

Chapter 5: Introduction to Cloud Platforms

Cloud computing has revolutionized the way we build, deploy, and scale applications. It offers a flexible and scalable infrastructure that can be accessed over the internet.

Major Cloud Providers

There are three major cloud providers dominating the market:

1. AMAZON WEB SERVICES (AWS): The pioneer in cloud computing, offering a wide range of services, including compute, storage, databases, analytics, machine learning, and more.

2. MICROSOFT AZURE: A comprehensive cloud platform providing a wide range of services, including compute, storage, databases, analytics, AI, and IoT.

3. GOOGLE CLOUD PLATFORMS (GCP): A powerful cloud platform offering a range of services, including compute, storage, databases, machine learning, and big data analytics.

Core Cloud Services

1. Compute Services:

- Virtual Machines (VMs): Virtualized servers that can be customized to run specific applications.
- Serverless Computing: A computing execution model where the cloud provider automatically manages the allocation of machine resources.
- Container Services: Platforms for deploying and managing containerized applications.

2. Storage Services:

- Object Storage: Stores large amounts of unstructured data, such as images, videos, and documents.
- Block Storage: Provides raw block-level storage for applications that require high performance and low latency.
- File Storage: Offers file-based storage for sharing and accessing files from multiple devices.

3. Database Services:
- Relational Databases: Traditional databases that store data in tables.
- NoSQL Databases: Databases that store data in a non-tabular format, suitable for large-scale, high-performance applications.
- Data Warehouses and Data Lakes: Platforms for storing and analyzing large amounts of data.

4. Networking Services:
- Virtual Private Clouds (VPCs): Isolated virtual networks within a cloud provider's infrastructure.
- Load Balancing: Distributes incoming traffic across multiple servers to improve performance and reliability.
- Content Delivery Networks (CDNs): Delivers content to users globally with low latency.

Choosing the Right Cloud Platform
When selecting a cloud platform, consider the following factors:

- Scalability: The ability to scale resources up or down to meet changing demands.
- Performance: The speed and responsiveness of the platform.
- Security: The level of security and compliance features offered.
- Cost: The pricing model and cost-effectiveness of the platform.
- Integration: The ease of integrating with existing systems and tools.
- Support: The quality of technical support provided by the cloud provider.

With these core concepts and benefits of cloud computing, you can leverage these platforms to build scalable, reliable, and cost-effective applications.

Major Cloud Providers: AWS, GCP, and Azure

The cloud computing landscape is dominated by three major players: Amazon Web Services (AWS), Google Cloud Platform (GCP), and Microsoft Azure. Each provider offers a comprehensive suite of services to meet diverse cloud computing needs.

Amazon Web Services (AWS)

As the pioneer in cloud computing, AWS offers a vast array of services, including:
- Compute Services: EC2 (Elastic Compute Cloud), Lambda (serverless computing)
- Storage Services: S3 (Simple Storage Service), EBS (Elastic Block Store)
- Database Services: RDS (Relational Database Service), DynamoDB (NoSQL database)
- Networking Services: VPC (Virtual Private Cloud), Route 53 (DNS service)
- Analytics Services: Redshift (data warehouse), EMR (Elastic MapReduce)
- Machine Learning Services: SageMaker, Rekognition

Google Cloud Platform (GCP)

GCP provides a robust and scalable cloud platform, with a focus on data analytics and machine learning:
- Compute Services: Compute Engine, App Engine, Functions
- Storage Services: Cloud Storage, Persistent Disk
- Database Services: Cloud SQL, BigQuery, Firestore
- Networking Services: Virtual Private Cloud, Cloud Load Balancing
- Data Analytics Services: BigQuery, Dataflow
- Machine Learning Services: AI Platform, AutoML

Microsoft Azure

Azure offers a comprehensive cloud platform with a strong focus on hybrid and multi-cloud solutions:
- Compute Services: Virtual Machines, App Service, Functions
- Storage Services: Azure Storage, Azure Disk Storage
- Database Services: Azure SQL Database, Cosmos DB, Azure Database for PostgreSQL
- Networking Services: Virtual Networks, Azure Load Balancer
- Analytics Services: Azure Synapse Analytics, Azure Data Lake Analytics

- AI and Machine Learning Services: Azure Machine Learning, Azure Cognitive Services

Choosing the Right Cloud Provider
The choice of cloud provider depends on various factors, including:
- Workload requirements: The specific needs of your application, such as compute power, storage capacity, and database requirements.
- Existing infrastructure: Compatibility with your existing on-premises infrastructure.
- Cost: The pricing models and cost-effectiveness of each provider.
- Security and compliance: The security features and compliance certifications offered by each provider.
- Developer expertise: The level of familiarity and experience with the provider's tools and services.

Core Cloud Services: Compute, Storage, and Networking

Cloud computing offers a wide range of services, but three core services form the foundation of most cloud-based applications: compute, storage, and networking.

Compute Services
Compute services provide the processing power needed to run applications. They allow you to rent virtual machines or use serverless functions to execute your code.

Virtual Machines (VMs):
- Virtualized servers that can be customized to run specific applications.
- You have control over the operating system, software, and configuration.
- Suitable for applications with specific hardware or software requirements.

Serverless Computing:
- A computing execution model where the cloud provider automatically manages the allocation of machine resources.

- You only pay for the compute time consumed by your functions
- Ideal for event-driven applications and microservices.

Storage Services
- Storage services provide the ability to store and retrieve data. They offer various storage options to meet different needs, such as object storage, block storage, and file storage.

Object Storage:
- Stores large amounts of unstructured data, such as images, videos, and documents.
- Highly scalable and durable.
- Ideal for storing backups, media assets, and data lakes.

Block Storage:
- Provides raw block-level storage for applications that require high performance and low latency.
- Often used for boot volumes and data disks for virtual machines.

File Storage:
- Offers file-based storage for sharing and accessing files from multiple devices.
- Suitable for storing configuration files, application code, and user data.

Networking Services
Networking services enable communication between different components of a cloud-based application. They provide a variety of network functionalities, such as virtual private clouds, load balancing, and content delivery networks.

Virtual Private Clouds (VPCs):
- Isolated virtual networks within a cloud provider's infrastructure.
- You can create subnets, route traffic, and configure security groups within your VPC.

Load Balancing:
- Distributes incoming traffic across multiple servers to improve performance and reliability.

- Can be used to balance traffic based on various criteria, such as round robin, least connections, or weighted round robin.

Content Delivery Networks (CDNs):
- Delivers content to users globally with low latency.
- Caches content at edge locations to reduce network latency and improve performance.

Choosing the Right Cloud Platform for Your Needs

When selecting a cloud provider, several factors should be considered:

1. Workload Requirements:
- Compute-intensive workloads: If your applications demand significant processing power, consider providers like AWS EC2 or Google Compute Engine.
- Data-intensive workloads: For handling large datasets, platforms like AWS S3 or Google Cloud Storage are ideal.
- Real-time applications: Serverless functions like AWS Lambda or Google Cloud Functions are well-suited for real-time processing and event-driven architectures.

2. Security and Compliance:
- Data security: Evaluate the provider's security measures, such as encryption, access controls, and security certifications.
- Compliance: Ensure the provider meets industry-specific compliance standards (e.g., HIPAA, GDPR, PCI DSS).
- Data residency: Consider where your data will be stored and the relevant data sovereignty regulations.

3. Cost:
- Pricing models: Compare the pricing models offered by different providers, including pay-as-you-go, reserved instances, and spot instances.
- Cost optimization: Utilize cost optimization tools and strategies to minimize expenses.

- Long-term commitment: Consider the potential cost savings of long-term contracts or commitments.

4. Scalability and Performance:
- Scalability: Assess the provider's ability to scale resources up or down to meet fluctuating demands.
- Performance Evaluate the performance metrics, such as latency, throughput, and network bandwidth.
- Global reach: Consider the provider's global infrastructure and data center locations for optimal performance.

5. Developer Tools and Support:
- Developer tools: Assess the availability of developer tools, SDKs, and APIs.
- Support: Evaluate the quality and responsiveness of the provider's technical support.
- Community and documentation: Consider the size and activity of the provider's community and the availability of documentation and tutorials.

6. Vendor Lock-In:
- Portability: Evaluate the ease of migrating workloads to another provider.
- Open-source technologies: Consider using open-source tools and frameworks to reduce vendor lock-in.

By considering these factors, you can select the cloud platform that best aligns with your specific needs and goals.

PART III: BUILDING INTELLIGENT APPLICATIONS WITH SERVERLESS MACHINE LEARNING

Chapter 6: Data Preparation and Feature Engineering

Data preparation and feature engineering are crucial steps in the machine learning pipeline. They involve transforming raw data into a suitable format for model training.

Data Collection and Sources

Data is the fuel that drives machine learning models. The quality and quantity of data significantly impact the performance of a model. Here are some common sources for data collection:

Public Datasets

Numerous public datasets are available for machine learning research and experimentation. These datasets are often curated and cleaned, making them ideal for beginners.

- UCI Machine Learning Repository: A popular repository for various machine learning datasets.
- Kaggle: A platform for data science competitions and datasets.
- Google Dataset Search: A search engine for finding datasets across the web.

Web Scraping

Web scraping involves extracting data from websites. Tools like BeautifulSoup and Scrapy can be used to automate this process. However, it's important to respect website terms of service and avoid overloading servers.

APIs

Many services provide APIs to access their data. For example, you can use the Twitter API to collect tweets or the Google Books API to access book information.

Sensors

IoT devices and sensors generate a wealth of data, including temperature, humidity, and location data. This data can be collected and analyzed to gain valuable insights.

Databases

Databases store structured data, such as customer information, sales data, and financial records. SQL and NoSQL databases are commonly used to store and retrieve data.

Key Considerations for Data Collection:
- Data Quality: Ensure data accuracy, completeness, and consistency.
- Data Quantity: Collect sufficient data to train effective models.
- Data Relevance: Collect data that is relevant to the problem you want to solve.
- Data Privacy and Ethics: Adhere to data privacy regulations and ethical guidelines.
- Data Bias: Be aware of biases in the data and take steps to mitigate them.

Data Cleaning and Preprocessing

Real-world data is often messy and incomplete. Data cleaning and preprocessing are essential steps to ensure the quality and consistency of the data before feeding it into a machine learning model.

Common Data Cleaning and Preprocessing Techniques

Handling Missing Values
- Deletion: Remove rows or columns with missing values.
- Imputation: Fill missing values with statistical measures like mean, median, or mode.
- Prediction: Use machine learning models to predict missing values.

Outlier Detection and Handling
- Statistical Methods: Use techniques like Z-score or IQR to identify outliers.
- Visualization: Visualize data to identify outliers visually.

- Handling Outliers: Remove, cap, or impute outliers based on the specific context.

Data Normalization and Standardization
- Normalization: Scales numerical features to a specific range (e.g., 0-1).
- Standardization: Scales numerical features to have zero mean and unit variance.

Categorical Data Encoding
- One-Hot Encoding: Creates binary features for each category.
- Label Encoding: Assigns numerical labels to categories.

Text Data Preprocessing
- Tokenization: Breaking text into words or tokens.
- Stop Word Removal: Removing common words that don't add much meaning.
- Stemming and Lemmatization: Reducing words to their root form.
- Text Vectorization: Converting text into numerical representations.

Feature Engineering
- Feature Creation: Creating new features from existing ones.
- Feature Selection: Selecting the most relevant features.

Data Quality Assessment
Data Validation: Ensuring data conforms to specific rules and constraints.
Data Consistency: Checking for inconsistencies and errors in the data.

Feature Extraction and Selection

Feature engineering is a critical step in the machine learning pipeline. It involves creating new features or transforming existing ones to improve model performance.

Feature Extraction

Feature extraction involves transforming raw data into a set of features that are more informative and relevant to the machine learning task.

Common Feature Extraction Techniques:

Text Data:
- Bag-of-Words: Converts text into a bag of words, ignoring word order.
- TF-IDF: Weights words based on their frequency and importance.
- Word Embeddings: Represents words as dense vectors in a semantic space.

Image Data:
- Convolutional Neural Networks (CNNs): Automatically learn features from images.
- Principal Component Analysis (PCA): Reduces dimensionality while preserving most of the variance.

Time Series Data:
- Time Series Decomposition: Breaks down time series into trend, seasonal, and residual components.
- Fourier Transform: Converts time domain signals to frequency domain.
- Wavelet Transform: Represents signals in both time and frequency domains.

Feature Selection
Feature selection involves identifying the most relevant features to improve model performance and reduce overfitting.

Common Feature Selection Techniques:

Filter Methods:
- Correlation Analysis: Identifies features that are highly correlated with the target variable.
- Chi-Square Test: Measures the statistical significance of the relationship between categorical features and the target variable.
- Mutual Information: Measures the dependency between features and the target variable.

Wrapper Methods:
- Forward Selection: Iteratively adds features to the model, selecting the feature that improves performance the most.
- Backward Elimination: Iteratively removes features from the model, removing the feature that has the least impact on performance.
- Recursive Feature Elimination (RFE): Recursively removes features based on their importance scores.

Embedded Methods:
- Regularization Techniques: Penalize models with many features, effectively selecting the most important ones (e.g., L1 and L2 regularization).
- Tree-Based Methods: Feature importance scores can be derived from decision trees and random forests.

Data Transformation and Normalization

Data transformation and normalization are essential steps in the machine learning pipeline. They involve converting data into a suitable format for machine learning algorithms.

Data Transformation

Data transformation involves converting data from one format to another. This is often necessary to make data more suitable for analysis and modeling.

Common Data Transformation Techniques:

Text Data:
- Tokenization: Breaking text into words or tokens.
- Stemming and Lemmatization: Reducing words to their root form.
- Text Vectorization: Converting text into numerical representations.

Time Series Data:
- Time Series Decomposition: Breaking down time series into trend, seasonal, and residual components.
- Fourier Transform: Converting time domain signals to frequency domain.
- Wavelet Transform: Representing signals in both time and frequency domains.

Categorical Data Encoding:
- One-Hot Encoding: Creating binary features for each category.
- Label Encoding: Assigning numerical labels to categories.

Data Normalization

Data normalization is a technique used to scale numerical features to a specific range. This can help improve the performance of machine learning algorithms.

Common Normalization Techniques:

Min-Max Scaling: Scales features to a specific range (e.g., 0-1).

```python
X_scaled = (X - X.min()) / (X.max() - X.min())
```

* **Standardization:** Scales features to have zero mean and unit variance.
```python
X_scaled = (X - X.mean()) / X.std()
```

Why Normalization is Important:

- Improved Model Performance: Many machine learning algorithms assume that features are on a similar scale. Normalization helps to ensure that features are treated equally.
- Faster Convergence: Normalization can help gradient descent algorithms converge faster.
- Better Visualization: Normalized data can be visualized more effectively.

With all these, you can easily improve the accuracy and performance of your machine learning models.

Chapter 7: Model Training and Evaluation

Once the data is cleaned, preprocessed, and transformed, the next step is to train a machine learning model. Model training involves feeding the prepared data to an algorithm to learn patterns and relationships.

Choosing the Right Algorithm

Selecting the appropriate algorithm is a critical step in the machine learning pipeline. The choice of algorithm depends on various factors, including the type of problem, the size and quality of the data, and the desired level of accuracy and interpretability.

Key Factors to Consider:

1. Type of Problem:
- Regression: Predicting a continuous numerical value.
- Linear Regression: For linear relationships between features and the target variable.
- Polynomial Regression: For nonlinear relationships.
- Decision Tree Regression: For complex, nonlinear relationships.
- Classification: Categorizing data into discrete classes.
- Logistic Regression: For binary classification.
- Decision Trees: For both classification and regression.
- Random Forest: An ensemble of decision trees.
- Support Vector Machines (SVM): For complex classification tasks, especially with high-dimensional data.
- Naive Bayes: For text classification and spam filtering.
- Clustering: Grouping similar data points together.
- K-Means Clustering: For partitioning data into K clusters.
- Hierarchical Clustering: Creates a hierarchy of clusters.
- Anomaly Detection: Identifying outliers or anomalies.
- Isolation Forest: Isolates anomalies by randomly partitioning data.
- One-Class SVM: Defines a boundary around normal data points.

2. Data Characteristics:
- Size: For large datasets, consider scalable algorithms like decision trees, random forests, or neural networks.
- Complexity: For complex relationships, neural networks or deep learning models may be suitable.
- Noise: For noisy data, consider robust algorithms like decision trees or random forests.

3. Computational Resources:
- Consider the available computational power and memory when selecting algorithms.
- Some algorithms, such as deep learning models, require significant computational resources.

4. Interpretability:
- If interpretability is important, decision trees and linear regression models are good choices.
- Neural networks and complex ensemble models may be less interpretable.

It's important to note that the best way to determine the optimal algorithm for a specific problem is through experimentation and evaluation. You can use techniques like cross-validation to assess the performance of different algorithms on a given dataset.

By carefully considering these factors and experimenting with different algorithms, you can build effective machine learning models that solve real-world problems.

Model Training and Hyperparameter Tuning

Model Training

Model training involves feeding the prepared data to a machine learning algorithm. The algorithm learns from the data and adjusts its internal parameters to minimize the error between its predictions and the actual values.

Key Steps in Model Training:

1. Data Preparation: Ensure the data is cleaned, preprocessed, and transformed into a suitable format.
2. Model Initialization: Initialize the model's parameters randomly or using specific techniques.
3. Forward Pass: Feed the input data to the model to generate predictions.
4. Loss Calculation: Compute the difference between the predicted values and the actual values.
5. Backpropagation: Propagate the error back through the model's layers to update the parameters.
6. Parameter Update: Adjust the model's parameters using an optimization algorithm like gradient descent.
7. Repeat Steps 3-6: Iterate the process until the model converges or reaches a predefined number of epochs.

Hyperparameter Tuning

Hyperparameters are parameters that are set before the training process begins and control the learning process and the complexity of the model.

Common Hyperparameters:

- Learning Rate: Determines the step size during optimization.
- Number of Iterations: The number of times the algorithm iterates over the training data.
- Regularization: A technique to prevent overfitting.
- Number of Hidden Layers and Neurons: In neural networks, these parameters control the model's complexity.

Hyperparameter Tuning Techniques:

- Grid Search: Evaluates all possible combinations of hyperparameters within a specified range.
- Random Search: Randomly samples hyperparameter values.
- Bayesian Optimization: Uses Bayesian statistics to intelligently explore the hyperparameter space.

Evaluation Metrics:

- Accuracy: Proportion of correct predictions.
- Precision: Proportion of positive predictions that are correct.
- Recall: Proportion of actual positive cases that are correctly identified.
- F1-Score: Harmonic mean of precision and recall.
- Confusion Matrix: A table that summarizes the performance of a classification model.
- Mean Squared Error (MSE): Measures the average squared difference between predicted and actual values.
- Root Mean Squared Error (RMSE): The square root of MSE.
- Mean Absolute Error (MAE): The average absolute difference between predicted and actual values.

Model Evaluation Metrics

Model evaluation metrics are crucial for assessing the performance of a machine learning model. They help determine how well a model generalizes to new, unseen data. Here are some common evaluation metrics:

Classification Metrics
- Accuracy: The proportion of correct predictions.
- Precision: The proportion of positive predictions that are correct.
- Recall: The proportion of actual positive cases that are correctly identified.
- F1-Score: The harmonic mean of precision and recall.
- Confusion Matrix: A table that summarizes the performance of a classification model.

Regression Metrics
- Mean Squared Error (MSE): Measures the average squared difference between predicted and actual values.
- Root Mean Squared Error (RMSE): The square root of MSE.
- Mean Absolute Error (MAE): The average absolute difference between predicted and actual values.
- R-squared: Measures the proportion of variance in the dependent variable explained by the independent variables.

Other Metrics

- Log Loss: Measures the performance of classification models.
- ROC Curve: Visualizes the trade-off between true positive rate and false positive rate.
- AUC-ROC: Area Under the Curve of the ROC curve.

Choosing the Right Metrics:

The choice of evaluation metric depends on the specific problem and the desired outcome. For example:

- Imbalanced Datasets: Precision, recall, and F1-score are more informative than accuracy.
- Regression Problems: MSE, RMSE, and MAE are commonly used.
- Ranking Problems: Mean Average Precision (MAP) and Normalized Discounted Cumulative Gain (NDCG) are used.

Additional Considerations:

- Cross-Validation: A technique to assess model performance on different subsets of the data.
- Hyperparameter Tuning: Optimize hyperparameters to improve model performance.
- Overfitting and Underfitting: Avoid overfitting by using regularization techniques and underfitting by increasing model complexity.

Model Selection and Ensemble Methods

Model Selection

Selecting the right machine learning model is crucial for achieving optimal performance. Several factors influence this decision, including:

- Problem Type: Is it a classification, regression, clustering, or anomaly detection problem?
- Data Characteristics: Size, complexity, and noise level of the data.
- Computational Resources: Available computational power and memory.
- Interpretability: The need to understand the model's decision-making process.

Ensemble Methods

Ensemble methods combine multiple models to improve overall performance. By combining diverse models, ensemble methods can reduce bias, variance, and overfitting.

Common Ensemble Methods:

1. Bagging:
- Trains multiple models on different subsets of the training data.
- Reduces variance and improves stability.
- Random Forest: A popular bagging ensemble that uses decision trees as base models.

2. Boosting:
- Sequentially trains models, with each model focusing on correcting the errors of the previous models.
- Reduces bias and improves accuracy.
- Gradient Boosting: A powerful boosting technique that iteratively trains models to minimize the loss function.
- AdaBoost: Adaptively weights training samples to focus on difficult examples.
- XGBoost: A scalable and efficient implementation of gradient boosting.

3. Stacking:
- Combines multiple models by training a meta-model to learn how to best combine their predictions.
- Can improve performance by leveraging the strengths of different models.

Key Considerations for Ensemble Methods:
- Diversity: Ensure that the base models are diverse to avoid overfitting.
- Bias-Variance Trade-off: Balance the trade-off between bias and variance.
- Computational Cost: Ensemble methods can be computationally expensive, especially for large datasets.

By carefully selecting models and considering ensemble methods, you can build robust and accurate machine learning systems.

Chapter 8: Deploying Machine Learning Models Serverlessly

Serverless computing offers a powerful and efficient way to deploy machine learning models. By leveraging serverless platforms, you can automatically scale your applications, reduce operational overhead, and focus on building and deploying models.

Model Deployment Strategies

Model deployment is the final step in the machine learning pipeline, where the trained model is deployed into a production environment to make predictions or decisions. There are several strategies for deploying machine learning models, each with its own advantages and disadvantages.

1. Batch Inference

Suitable for: Batch processing of large datasets.
Process:
- Collect a batch of data.
- Feed the batch to the model.
- Process the batch and generate predictions.

Platforms:
- Cloud platforms like AWS Batch, Google Cloud Dataproc, and Azure Batch.
- Serverless functions like AWS Lambda, Google Cloud Functions, and Azure Functions.

2. Real-time Inference

Suitable for: Low-latency applications like recommendation systems, fraud detection, and real-time analytics.
Process:
- Receive a request with input data.
- Process the input data and feed it to the model.
- Generate predictions and return the results.

Platforms:
- REST APIs: Expose the model as a REST API using frameworks like Flask or FastAPI.

- Real-time streaming platforms: Use platforms like Kafka or Kinesis to process real-time data streams.
- Serverless functions: Deploy models as serverless functions to handle real-time requests efficiently.

3. Model Serving Frameworks
- MLflow: A platform for managing the entire machine learning lifecycle, including deployment.
- TensorFlow Serving: A flexible platform for deploying TensorFlow models.
- TorchServe: A platform for deploying PyTorch models.
- Kubeflow: A platform for building and deploying machine learning pipelines on Kubernetes.

Key Considerations for Model Deployment
- Performance: Ensure the model can handle the required load and latency.
- Scalability: The ability to handle increasing workloads.
- Security: Protect the model and data from unauthorized access.
- Monitoring: Monitor the model's performance and retrain as needed.
- Cost-Efficiency: Optimize resource utilization to minimize costs.
- Reliability: Ensure high availability and fault tolerance.

Serverless Deployment with AWS Lambda and API Gateway

AWS Lambda and API Gateway are powerful tools for deploying machine learning models serverlessly. This approach offers several benefits, including automatic scaling, pay-per-use pricing, and reduced operational overhead.

Steps to Deploy a Machine Learning Model with AWS Lambda and API Gateway:

1. Package the Model:
- Create a deployment package containing the model artifacts (e.g., model weights, configuration files) and the necessary dependencies.
- The package should be compatible with the Lambda runtime environment (e.g., Python, Node.js, Java).

2. Create a Lambda Function:
- Use the AWS Management Console, AWS CLI, or SDKs to create a Lambda function.
- Configure the function's runtime environment, memory allocation, and timeout settings.
- Upload the deployment package to the Lambda function.
- Write a handler function that takes input data, makes predictions using the model, and returns the results.

3. Create an API Gateway:
- Set up an API Gateway to expose the Lambda function as an HTTP endpoint.
- Configure API Gateway to handle incoming requests, authenticate users, and route requests to the Lambda function.
- Define API methods (e.g., GET, POST) and specify input and output parameters.

4. Test and Deploy:
- Test the API endpoint to ensure the model is working correctly.
- Deploy the API to production.

Key Considerations for Serverless Deployment:
- Cold Start: Lambda functions have a cold start time, which is the time taken to initialize the function's environment. To minimize cold start time, consider using provisioned concurrency or warming up the function.
- Model Size and Complexity: Large and complex models can impact performance and cost. Optimize model size and consider using techniques like model quantization or pruning.
- Concurrency Limits: AWS Lambda has limits on the number of concurrent executions. For high-traffic applications, consider using techniques like batching or asynchronous processing.
- Security: Implement appropriate security measures, such as IAM roles, API keys, and encryption, to protect your model and data.

- Monitoring and Logging: Monitor the performance of your deployed model and use logging to troubleshoot issues.

Serverless Deployment with Google Cloud Functions and Cloud Run

Google Cloud Platform offers two primary services for serverless deployment: Cloud Functions and Cloud Run.

Google Cloud Functions
- Event-Driven: Triggered by events like HTTP requests, database changes, or messages from other services.
- Scalability: Automatically scales to handle varying workloads.
- Pay-Per-Use: You only pay for the compute time consumed by your functions.

Deployment Steps:

1. Create a Cloud Function:
- Define the function's trigger (e.g., HTTP request, Pub/Sub message).
- Write the function's code in supported languages like Python, Node.js, Java, or Go.
- Deploy the function to a region.

2. Package the Model:
- Package the model and its dependencies into a container image.

3. Deploy the Model:
- Upload the container image to Google Container Registry.
- Configure the Cloud Function to use the container image.

Google Cloud Run
- Container-Based: Deploy containerized applications without managing servers.
- Fully Managed: Google Cloud handles the infrastructure and scaling.

- Custom Domains and SSL: Support for custom domains and SSL certificates.

Deployment Steps:

1. Package the Model:
- Create a container image containing the model and its dependencies.

2. Deploy the Model:
- Deploy the container image to Cloud Run.
- Configure the service's scaling settings, memory limits, and network settings.

Key Considerations for Serverless Deployment on GCP:
- Cold Start: Cloud Functions have a cold start time, which can impact performance. Consider using background functions to minimize cold starts.
- Memory and Timeout Limits: Be aware of the memory and timeout limits for Cloud Functions and Cloud Run.
- Cost Optimization: Optimize resource usage to minimize costs.
- Security: Implement appropriate security measures, such as authentication, authorization, and encryption.
- Monitoring and Logging: Use Cloud Monitoring and Logging to monitor the performance and health of your deployed models.

Serverless Deployment with Azure Functions and Azure App Service

Azure offers two primary services for serverless deployment: Azure Functions and Azure App Service.

Azure Functions
- Event-Driven: Triggered by events like HTTP requests, timer triggers, or messages from other services.
- Scalability: Automatically scales to handle varying workloads.

- Pay-Per-Use: You only pay for the compute time consumed by your functions.

Deployment Steps:

1. Create an Azure Function:
- Choose a trigger type (e.g., HTTP trigger, timer trigger).
- Write the function's code in supported languages like C#, JavaScript, or Python.
- Deploy the function to an Azure Function App.

2. Package the Model:
- Package the model and its dependencies as a deployment package.

3. Deploy the Model:
- Deploy the package to the Azure Function App.
- Configure the function to load the model and make predictions.

Azure App Service
- Container-Based: Deploy containerized applications without managing servers.
- Fully Managed: Azure handles the infrastructure and scaling.
- Custom Domains and SSL: Support for custom domains and SSL certificates.

Deployment Steps:

1. Package the Model:
- Create a container image containing the model and its dependencies.

2. Deploy the Model:
- Deploy the container image to Azure App Service.
- Configure the app service's scaling settings, memory limits, and network settings.

Key Considerations for Serverless Deployment on Azure:

- Cold Start: Azure Functions have a cold start time, which can impact performance. Consider using pre-warmed instances or background functions to minimize cold starts.
- Cost Optimization: Optimize resource usage to minimize costs.
- Security: Implement appropriate security measures, such as authentication, authorization, and encryption.
- Monitoring and Logging: Use Azure Monitor to monitor the performance and health of your deployed models.

By leveraging Azure Functions and Azure App Service, you can efficiently deploy machine learning models to production, enabling real-time predictions and scalable applications.

Chapter 9: Building Real-World Applications

Now that we've covered the fundamental concepts and techniques of machine learning and serverless computing, let's dive into building real-world applications. In this chapter, we'll explore several practical examples of how to apply these technologies to solve real-world problems.

Image Classification with TensorFlow and AWS Lambda

Understanding the Problem

Image classification involves categorizing images into predefined classes. This task has a wide range of applications, including:

- Medical Image Analysis: Diagnosing diseases like cancer or identifying abnormalities.
- Self-Driving Cars: Recognizing objects like traffic signs, pedestrians, and other vehicles.
- Product Image Search:Visual search engines that allow users to search for products using images.

Building the Image Classification Model

1. Data Collection and Preparation:
- Gather a large dataset of images labeled with their corresponding classes.
- Preprocess the images: Resize, normalize, and augment the images to improve model performance.

2. Model Architecture:
- Choose a suitable neural network architecture:** Convolutional Neural Networks (CNNs) are well-suited for image classification tasks.
- Design the network: Create a CNN with multiple convolutional layers, pooling layers, and fully connected layers.

3. Model Training:

- Compile the model: Define the loss function (e.g., categorical cross-entropy) and optimizer (e.g., Adam, SGD).
- Train the model: Feed the preprocessed images and their corresponding labels to the model.
- Monitor the training process: Track metrics like accuracy, loss, and validation accuracy.

4. Model Evaluation:
- Evaluate the model's performance: Use metrics like accuracy, precision, recall, and F1-score.
- Consider techniques like cross-validation to get a more reliable estimate of the model's performance.

Deploying the Model to AWS Lambda

1. Export the Model:
- Save the trained model in a format compatible with TensorFlow Serving or TensorFlow Lite.

2. Create a Lambda Function:
- Write a Lambda function that takes an image as input and loads the exported model.
- Preprocess the image: Resize, normalize, and convert it to the expected input format.
- Make predictions: Use the loaded model to make predictions on the preprocessed image.
- Return the predicted class as the function's output.

3. Create an API Gateway:
- Set up an API Gateway to expose the Lambda function as an HTTP endpoint.
- Configure the API Gateway: Define the endpoint's URL, request and response formats, and authentication mechanisms.

Optimizing for Serverless Deployment

Model Optimization:
- Quantization: Reduce model size and improve inference speed.
- Pruning: Remove unnecessary weights and connections.
- Knowledge Distillation: Transfer knowledge from a large model to a smaller one.

Lambda Function Optimization:
- Choose appropriate memory and timeout settings.
- Use batch processing to improve efficiency and reduce costs.
- Warm up the function to minimize cold start time.

Natural Language Processing with Hugging Face and Google Cloud Functions

Natural Language Processing (NLP) is a field of artificial intelligence that focuses on the interaction between computers and human language. It involves tasks like text classification, sentiment analysis, machine translation, and text generation.

Understanding the Problem

In NLP, we often deal with unstructured text data. The goal is to extract meaningful information from this data. For example, we might want to:

- Classify text: Determine the sentiment of a review or the topic of an article.
- Generate text: Create human-quality text, such as product descriptions or news articles.
- Translate text: Translate text from one language to another.
- Extract information: Extract specific information from text, such as names, dates, or locations.

Leveraging Hugging Face

Hugging Face is a popular platform for NLP, providing a wide range of pre-trained models and tools. It offers a user-friendly interface and API to access and utilize these models.

Key benefits of using Hugging Face:
- Pre-trained models: Access state-of-the-art models for various NLP tasks.
- Easy-to-use API: Simple integration into your applications.
- Active community: Benefit from a large and active community of NLP practitioners.

Deploying NLP Models with Google Cloud Functions

Google Cloud Functions is a serverless computing platform that allows you to deploy functions triggered by events. This makes it an ideal platform for deploying NLP models.

Steps to deploy an NLP model with Google Cloud Functions:

1. Choose a pre-trained model: Select a suitable model from Hugging Face's model hub.
2. Package the model: Create a container image containing the model and its dependencies.
3. Deploy the model to Cloud Functions: Deploy the container image as a Cloud Function.
4. Trigger the function: Trigger the function using HTTP requests or Pub/Sub messages.

Example: Sentiment Analysis

1. Choose a pre-trained sentiment analysis model: Use a model like BERT or RoBERTa.
2. Create a Cloud Function: Write a function that takes text as input, passes it to the pre-trained model, and returns the predicted sentiment.
3. Deploy the function: Deploy the function to Cloud Functions.
4. Trigger the function: Use an HTTP request or a Pub/Sub message to trigger the function and get the sentiment analysis results.

Understanding Text Generation

Text generation involves creating human-quality text. This can be used for various applications such as:

- Creative Writing: Generating poems, scripts, or code.
- Chatbots: Creating more natural and engaging conversations.
- Content Generation: Auto-generating articles, reports, or product descriptions.

Using Hugging Face's Transformers Library

Hugging Face's Transformers library provides a wide range of pre-trained models for various NLP tasks, including text generation.

Key models for text generation:

- GPT-2: A powerful language model capable of generating coherent and contextually relevant text.
- GPT-3: An even more advanced language model, capable of generating highly realistic text.
- T5: A text-to-text transfer transformer, which can be used for various tasks, including text generation.

Deploying a Text Generation Model with Google Cloud Functions

1. Choose a pre-trained model: Select a suitable model from Hugging Face's model hub.
2. Package the model: Create a container image containing the model and its dependencies.
3. Deploy the model to Cloud Functions: Deploy the container image as a Cloud Function.
4. Trigger the function: Trigger the function using an HTTP request or a Pub/Sub message.

Example: Generating Text Prompts
1. Create a Cloud Function: Write a function that takes a prompt as input and generates text using the chosen pre-trained model.
2. Deploy the function: Deploy the function to Cloud Functions.

3. Trigger the function: Use an HTTP request to send a prompt to the function. The function will process the prompt and return generated text.

Key Considerations for Text Generation
- Model Selection: Choose a model that is suitable for the specific task and computational resources.
- Prompt Engineering: Carefully craft prompts to guide the model's output.
- Ethical Considerations: Be aware of the potential biases and ethical implications of generated text.
- Model Fine-tuning: Fine-tune the model on specific datasets to improve performance.
- Latency and Cost: Optimize the model and deployment strategy for low latency and cost-effectiveness.

Time Series Forecasting with Prophet and Azure Functions

Understanding Time Series Forecasting
Time series forecasting involves analyzing historical data to predict future values. It's widely used in various domains, such as:

- Finance: Predicting stock prices, exchange rates, or sales.
- Meteorology: Forecasting weather patterns.
- Energy: Predicting energy consumption or production.
- Supply Chain: Forecasting demand for products.

Using Prophet for Time Series Forecasting
Prophet is an open-source library developed by Facebook's Core Data Science team. It's designed to make time series forecasting easy and accessible.

Key Features of Prophet:
- Handles Trend and Seasonality: Automatically detects and models trend and seasonal patterns.
- Handles Holidays: Incorporates the impact of holidays on time series data.
- Allows for Changepoint Detection: Identifies significant changes in the trend.

- Easy to Use: Provides a simple interface for training and forecasting.

Deploying Prophet Models with Azure Functions

Azure Functions is a serverless computing platform that allows you to build and deploy event-driven applications without managing infrastructure. It's ideal for deploying time series forecasting models.

Steps to Deploy a Prophet Model with Azure Functions:

1. Train the Model:
- Prepare your time series data.
- Train a Prophet model using the `Prophet` library.

2. Package the Model:
- Create a deployment package containing the trained model and its dependencies.

3. Create an Azure Function:
- Create a function triggered by a timer or HTTP request.
- The function should load the model, make forecasts, and return the results.

4. Deploy the Function:
- Deploy the function to Azure Functions.

5. Schedule the Function:
- Use Azure Functions' timer trigger to schedule the function to run periodically and update the forecasts.

Example: Forecasting Product Sales

1. Collect historical sales data: Gather data on product sales over time.

2. Train a Prophet model: Train a Prophet model on the historical data to capture trends and seasonality.

3. Deploy the model to Azure Functions: Create a function that uses the trained model to forecast future sales.

4. Schedule the function: Schedule the function to run daily or weekly to generate updated forecasts.

Key Considerations for Time Series Forecasting with Azure Functions:

- Data Quality: Ensure data accuracy and completeness.
- Feature Engineering: Create relevant features like holidays, promotions, and economic indicators.
- Model Evaluation: Use appropriate metrics like Mean Absolute Error (MAE), Mean Squared Error (MSE), and Root Mean Squared Error (RMSE) to evaluate model performance.
- Model Retraining: Regularly retrain the model with new data to improve accuracy.
- Monitoring and Alerting: Monitor the performance of the model and set up alerts for anomalies or significant deviations.

Recommendation Systems with Collaborative Filtering and AWS Lambda

Understanding Recommendation Systems

Recommendation systems are algorithms that suggest items or content to users based on their past behavior or preferences. They are widely used in various domains, such as e-commerce, entertainment, and social media.

Collaborative Filtering is a popular technique for building recommendation systems. It relies on the idea that users with similar preferences will like similar items.

Building a Collaborative Filtering Recommendation System

1. Data Collection and Preparation:
- Collect user-item interaction data, such as ratings or purchase history.
- Clean the data to handle missing values and outliers.

2. Model Training:
- User-Based Collaborative Filtering: Recommends items based on the similarity between users.
- Item-Based Collaborative Filtering: Recommends items based on the similarity between items.

- Hybrid Approaches: Combine user-based and item-based approaches for better performance.

3. Generating Recommendations:
- Calculate similarity scores between users or items.
- Use the similarity scores to predict ratings for unseen items.
- Rank the predicted ratings to generate recommendations.

Deploying the Recommendation System with AWS Lambda

1. Package the Model:
- Create a deployment package containing the trained model, its dependencies, and the recommendation logic.

2. Create a Lambda Function:
- Create a Lambda function that takes user and item information as input.
- Load the trained model within the function.
- Use the model to generate recommendations based on the input.

3. Create an API Gateway:
- Set up an API Gateway to expose the Lambda function as an HTTP endpoint.
- Configure the API Gateway to handle incoming requests and return recommendations.

4. Test and Deploy:
- Test the API endpoint to ensure it works correctly.
- Deploy the API to production.

Key Considerations for Deployment
- Model Size and Complexity: Consider the size and complexity of the model when deploying to Lambda. Large models may require more memory and longer cold start times.

- Real-time vs. Batch Processing: For real-time recommendations, use a low-latency deployment strategy. For batch processing, consider using Lambda functions triggered by events like S3 object uploads.
- Scalability: Ensure the Lambda function and API Gateway can handle increasing traffic.
- Cost Optimization: Use appropriate configuration settings (e.g., memory allocation, timeout) to optimize costs.

Additional Techniques and Considerations

- Hybrid Approaches: Combine collaborative filtering with content-based filtering or knowledge-based techniques to improve recommendation accuracy.
- Deep Learning: Use deep learning models like neural networks to learn complex patterns in user-item interactions.
- Cold-Start Problem: Address the cold-start problem by using content-based recommendations or hybrid approaches.
- Evaluation Metrics: Use metrics like precision, recall, F1-score, and Mean Average Precision (MAP) to evaluate the performance of the recommendation system.

By leveraging the power of AWS Lambda and advanced recommendation techniques, you can build scalable and effective recommendation systems to enhance user experience and drive business growth.

PART IV: ADVANCED TOPICS AND FUTURE TRENDS

Chapter 10: MLOps: The Practice of Machine Learning

MLOps, or Machine Learning Operations, is a set of practices that aim to deploy and maintain machine learning models in production reliably and efficiently. It involves a combination of software engineering, machine learning, and DevOps principles.

Key Components of MLOps

- Model Development: Building, training, and evaluating machine learning models.
- Model Deployment: Deploying models to production environments.
- Model Monitoring: Tracking model performance and identifying issues.
- Model Retraining: Retraining models as needed to maintain performance.
- Model Governance: Ensuring model fairness, ethics, and compliance.

MLOps Lifecycle

The MLOps lifecycle typically involves the following steps:

1. Data Ingestion: Collect and ingest data from various sources.
2. Data Preparation: Clean, preprocess, and transform the data.
3. Model Training: Train machine learning models using appropriate algorithms and techniques.
4. Model Evaluation: Evaluate the model's performance using relevant metrics.
5. Model Deployment: Deploy the model to a production environment.
6. Model Monitoring: Monitor the model's performance and identify issues.
7. Model Retraining: Retrain the model as needed to maintain performance.
8. Model Governance: Ensure the model is fair, ethical, and compliant with regulations.

MLOps Tools and Frameworks

Several tools and frameworks can help streamline the MLOps process:

- MLflow: A platform for managing the machine learning lifecycle, including experiment tracking, model registry, and deployment.
- Kubeflow: A platform for building and deploying machine learning pipelines on Kubernetes.
- Airflow: A platform for scheduling and orchestrating data pipelines.
- DVC (Data Version Control): A tool for version controlling data and models.
- Jenkins: A popular automation server for CI/CD pipelines.

Challenges in MLOps

- Data Drift: Changes in data distribution can impact model performance.
- Model Degradation: Models may degrade over time due to concept drift or data quality issues.
- Scalability: Scaling machine learning pipelines can be challenging.
- Monitoring and Alerting: Setting up effective monitoring and alerting systems.
- Model Governance: Ensuring fairness, ethics, and compliance.

Best Practices for MLOps

- Automate Everything: Automate as many steps as possible in the MLOps pipeline.
- Version Control: Use version control for code, data, and models.
- Monitor Model Performance: Continuously monitor the model's performance and identify issues.
- Retrain Models Regularly: Retrain models as needed to maintain performance.
- Collaborate Effectively: Foster collaboration between data scientists, engineers, and operations teams.
- Prioritize Security and Privacy: Implement strong security measures to protect sensitive data.

Model Deployment and Monitoring

Model Deployment

Model deployment is the process of making a trained machine learning model accessible for real-world use. This involves deploying the model to a production environment where it can receive input data, generate predictions, and serve those predictions to users or other systems.

Key Strategies for Model Deployment

1. Batch Inference:

- Suitable for large datasets that can be processed in batches.
- Involves collecting a batch of data, feeding it to the model, and processing it to generate predictions.
- Platforms: Cloud platforms like AWS Batch, Google Cloud Dataproc, and Azure Batch.

2. Real-time Inference:

- Suitable for applications that require low-latency predictions, such as recommendation systems, chatbots, and real-time analytics.
- Involves receiving input data, processing it, and generating predictions in real-time.
- Platforms: REST APIs, real-time streaming platforms like Kafka or Kinesis, and serverless functions.

3. Model Serving Frameworks:

- Provide a dedicated infrastructure for deploying and serving machine learning models.
- MLflow: A platform for managing the entire machine learning lifecycle, including deployment.
- TensorFlow Serving: A flexible platform for deploying TensorFlow models.
- TorchServe: A platform for deploying PyTorch models.

- Kubeflow: A platform for building and deploying machine learning pipelines on Kubernetes.

Considerations for Model Deployment

- Performance: Ensure the model can handle the required load and latency.
- Scalability: The ability to handle increasing workloads.
- Security: Protect the model and data from unauthorized access.
- Monitoring: Continuously monitor the model's performance and identify issues.
- Cost-Efficiency: Optimize resource utilization to minimize costs.
- Reliability: Ensure high availability and fault tolerance.

Model Monitoring

Model monitoring is a critical aspect of MLOps. It involves tracking the performance of a deployed model over time and identifying potential issues, such as:

- Data Drift: Changes in the distribution of input data.
- Model Degradation: A decline in the model's performance.
- Concept Drift: Changes in the underlying relationships between features and the target variable.

Key Monitoring Metrics:

- Model Performance: Accuracy, precision, recall, F1-score, and other relevant metrics.
- Data Quality: Data completeness, consistency, and quality.
- Infrastructure Health: Monitor the health of the infrastructure hosting the model.
- Latency: Measure the time taken to generate predictions.
- Error Rates: Track the frequency and types of errors.

Monitoring Techniques:

- Logging: Log important information about the model's behavior, such as input data, predictions, and errors.
- Metrics: Track key performance metrics and visualize them using dashboards.
- Alerting: Set up alerts for critical events, such as model performance degradation or infrastructure failures.
- A/B Testing: Compare the performance of different model versions.

Model Retraining and Continuous Improvement

Model Retraining

As data evolves and changes over time, machine learning models may become less accurate. To maintain their performance, it's crucial to retrain them periodically. Here are some common scenarios that necessitate model retraining:

- Data Drift: The distribution of input data changes significantly.
- Concept Drift: The underlying relationship between features and target variables changes.
- Performance Degradation: The model's performance starts to decline.

Steps Involved in Model Retraining:

1. Data Collection: Gather new data to incorporate into the training process.
2. Data Preparation: Clean, preprocess, and transform the new data.
3. Model Retraining: Retrain the model on the combined dataset of old and new data.
4. Model Evaluation: Evaluate the retrained model's performance on a validation set.
5. Model Deployment: Deploy the retrained model to the production environment.

Continuous Integration and Continuous Delivery (CI/CD) for MLOps

CI/CD pipelines automate the process of building, testing, and deploying machine learning models. By automating these steps, you can reduce the time it takes to deploy new models and improve the overall efficiency of the MLOps process.

Key Components of a CI/CD Pipeline for MLOps:

- Version Control: Use a version control system like Git to manage code, data, and models.
- Data Pipeline: Automate data ingestion, cleaning, and preprocessing.
- Model Training: Automate the training process, including hyperparameter tuning and model selection.
- Model Testing: Evaluate the model's performance on a validation set.
- Model Deployment: Deploy the model to a production environment.
- Monitoring: Monitor the model's performance and trigger retraining if necessary.

Challenges in Model Retraining and Continuous Improvement

- Data Quality: Ensuring the quality and consistency of new data.
- Model Complexity: Managing the complexity of large models and pipelines.
- Computational Resources: Meeting the computational requirements for training and deployment.
- Ethical Considerations: Addressing bias and fairness in models.
- Change Management: Managing the impact of model changes on downstream systems.

Model Governance and Ethics

Model governance and ethics are critical aspects of MLOps. They ensure that models are developed and deployed responsibly, ethically, and in compliance with regulations.

Key Considerations for Model Governance and Ethics:

1. Fairness and Bias:
- Identify and mitigate bias: Use techniques like fairness metrics and bias detection tools to identify and mitigate bias in the data and model.

- Ensure equitable treatment: Ensure that the model treats all users fairly, regardless of their demographic characteristics.

2. Transparency and Explainability:
- Model interpretability: Use techniques like feature importance analysis and SHAP values to understand the model's decision-making process.
- Documentation: Document the model development process, including data sources, preprocessing steps, and model architecture.

3. Security and Privacy:
- Data privacy: Protect sensitive data using encryption and access controls.
- Model security: Secure the model and its deployment environment to prevent unauthorized access.
- Adherence to regulations: Comply with data privacy regulations like GDPR and CCPA.

4. Accountability:
- Establish accountability: Assign responsibility for model development, deployment, and monitoring.
- Implement a review process: Regularly review models to ensure they are performing as expected.

MLOps Tools for Governance and Ethics
Several tools can help with model governance and ethics:

- AI Fairness 360: A toolkit for auditing and mitigating bias in machine learning models.
- What-If Tool: A tool for exploring how model predictions change with different input features.
- LIME (Local Interpretable Model-Agnostic Explanations): A technique for explaining individual predictions.
- SHAP (SHapley Additive exPlanations): A game-theoretic approach to explaining model predictions.

Best Practices for Model Governance and Ethics

- Establish a Model Governance Framework: Define clear policies, procedures, and roles for model development, deployment, and monitoring.
- Regularly Review and Update Models: Monitor model performance and retrain as needed to maintain accuracy and fairness.
- Document Model Development and Deployment: Document the entire MLOps pipeline, including data sources, preprocessing steps, model architecture, and deployment details.
- Collaborate with Stakeholders: Involve stakeholders from different departments to ensure alignment with business objectives and ethical considerations.
- Promote Transparency and Explainability: Make model decisions understandable and transparent to users.
- Prioritize Fairness and Bias Mitigation: Use techniques to identify and mitigate bias in models.

By following these principles and leveraging appropriate tools, organizations can build and deploy ethical and responsible machine learning models that drive positive impact.

Chapter 11: Ethical Considerations in AI and ML

As artificial intelligence and machine learning continue to advance, it's crucial to consider the ethical implications of these technologies. Ethical concerns arise from the potential for bias, discrimination, and misuse of AI systems.

Key Ethical Considerations

1.Bias and Fairness:

- Algorithmic Bias: AI algorithms can perpetuate societal biases present in training data.
- Fairness Metrics: Use metrics like fairness parity difference and equalized odds to evaluate model fairness.
- Data Diversity: Ensure that training data is diverse and representative.
- Regular Auditing: Regularly audit models for bias and take corrective actions.

2. Privacy and Security:

- Data Privacy: Protect user privacy by implementing strong data protection measures.
- Data Security: Secure sensitive data to prevent unauthorized access.
- Transparent Data Practices: Be transparent about data collection and usage.

3. Transparency and Explainability:

- Model Interpretability: Use techniques like LIME and SHAP to explain model decisions.
- Human Oversight: Ensure human oversight in critical decision-making processes.

4. Accountability and Responsibility:

- Accountability: Assign responsibility for AI systems and their outcomes.
- Ethical Guidelines: Develop and adhere to ethical guidelines for AI development and deployment.

Mitigating Ethical Risks

- Diverse and Inclusive Teams: Foster diverse teams to reduce bias in model development.
- Ethical Guidelines and Policies: Develop and enforce ethical guidelines and policies for AI development.
- Regular Audits and Assessments: Conduct regular audits to identify and address potential issues.
- Transparency and Explainability: Make AI systems transparent and explainable.
- User Education and Consent: Educate users about how AI systems work and obtain informed consent.
- Collaboration with Stakeholders: Engage with stakeholders to address ethical concerns and ensure responsible AI development.

Real-world Examples of Ethical Challenges

- Facial Recognition: Bias in facial recognition systems can lead to discriminatory outcomes.
- Autonomous Vehicles: Ethical dilemmas in decision-making, such as the trolley problem.
- Algorithmic Hiring: Bias in hiring algorithms can lead to unfair hiring practices.

Bias and Fairness in AI

Bias in AI refers to systematic errors in a model's predictions or decisions that are often a reflection of biases present in the training data or the algorithm itself. This can lead to unfair and discriminatory outcomes.

Sources of Bias in AI

Biased Data:
- Sampling Bias: The training data may not be representative of the population.

- Labeling Bias: Human biases can influence the labeling of data.
- Measurement Bias: Errors in measurement instruments or data collection processes.

Algorithmic Bias:
- Algorithmic Design: The algorithm itself may be biased.
- Feature Engineering: The selection and engineering of features can introduce bias.

Consequences of Bias in AI

- Unfair Decisions: Biased models can lead to unfair decisions, such as discriminatory hiring practices or biased loan approvals.
- Reduced Accuracy: Bias can reduce the accuracy and reliability of AI systems.
- Loss of Trust: Biased AI systems can erode public trust in AI and technology.

Mitigating Bias in AI

Fairness Metrics:
- Demographic Parity: Ensure that the model's predictions are equally distributed across different demographic groups.
- Equalized Odds: Ensure that the model's false positive and false negative rates are equal across different groups.
- Predictive Parity: Ensure that the model's positive predictive value is equal across different groups.

Data Quality and Diversity:
- Data Collection: Collect diverse and representative data.
- Data Cleaning: Remove biases and inconsistencies in the data.
- Data Augmentation: Generate synthetic data to increase diversity.

Algorithm Selection and Tuning:
- Choose Fair Algorithms: Select algorithms that are less prone to bias.

- Regularization: Use regularization techniques to prevent overfitting and reduce bias.
- Hyperparameter Tuning: Tune hyperparameters to minimize bias.

Model Interpretability:
- Explainable AI: Use techniques like LIME and SHAP to understand the model's decision-making process.
- Feature Importance Analysis: Identify the most important features and assess their potential for bias.

Continuous Monitoring and Evaluation:
- Monitor Model Performance: Regularly monitor the model's performance on different demographic groups.
- Retrain Models: Retrain models with new data to address evolving biases.

Privacy and Security Concerns

As AI and machine learning systems become increasingly sophisticated, so too do the privacy and security risks associated with them. These concerns are paramount, as they can impact individual privacy, societal trust in AI, and even national security.

Key Privacy and Security Concerns

1. Data Privacy:
- Data Collection: The collection of personal data, especially sensitive information, raises concerns about privacy.
- Data Storage: Storing large amounts of personal data poses risks of data breaches and unauthorized access.
- Data Sharing: Sharing data with third parties can lead to privacy violations.

2. Model Security:

- Adversarial Attacks: Malicious actors can manipulate input data to deceive AI models.
- Model Theft: Stolen models can be misused or reverse-engineered.
- Model Poisoning: Injecting malicious data into the training data to compromise the model.

3. Ethical Implications:
- Surveillance:AI-powered surveillance systems can raise concerns about privacy and civil liberties.
- Discrimination: Biased AI systems can lead to discriminatory outcomes.

Mitigating Privacy and Security Risks

1. Data Privacy:
- Data Minimization: Collect only the necessary data.
- Data Anonymization and Pseudonymization: Remove or mask personally identifiable information.
- Secure Data Storage: Implement robust security measures to protect data.
- Privacy by Design: Incorporate privacy considerations into the design of AI systems.

2. Model Security:
- Model Obfuscation: Make the model more difficult to understand and reverse-engineer.
- Adversarial Training: Train models to be robust against adversarial attacks.
- Secure Model Deployment: Deploy models securely, protecting them from unauthorized access.

3. Ethical Considerations:
- Transparency and Explainability: Make AI systems transparent and explainable.
- Fairness and Bias Mitigation: Implement measures to address bias and ensure fairness.
- Human Oversight: Ensure human oversight in critical decision-making processes.

Best Practices for Secure and Ethical AI

- Regular Security Audits: Conduct regular security audits to identify and address vulnerabilities.
- Data Privacy Compliance: Adhere to relevant data privacy regulations (e.g., GDPR, CCPA).
- Robust Access Controls: Implement strong access controls to limit access to sensitive data and models.
- Secure Model Deployment: Deploy models to secure environments with appropriate security measures.
- Continuous Monitoring: Monitor the performance of AI systems and detect anomalies.
- Ethical Guidelines: Develop and adhere to ethical guidelines for AI development and deployment.
- User Education and Consent: Educate users about the use of AI and obtain their informed consent.

Responsible AI and Societal Impact

As **AI** continues to advance, it's crucial to consider the broader societal implications of these technologies. Responsible AI involves developing and deploying AI systems that are ethical, fair, and beneficial to society.

Key Considerations for Responsible AI

Bias and Fairness:
- Algorithmic Bias: AI algorithms can perpetuate societal biases present in training data.
- Fairness Metrics: Use metrics like demographic parity, equalized odds, and predictive parity to assess fairness.
- Data Diversity: Ensure diverse and representative training data.

Transparency and Explainability:
- Model Interpretability: Use techniques like LIME and SHAP to explain model decisions.

- Human-in-the-Loop: Involve human experts to oversee and correct AI decisions.

Privacy and Security:
- Data Privacy: Protect user privacy by minimizing data collection and implementing strong security measures.
- Model Security: Secure AI models from attacks and unauthorized access.

Job Displacement and Economic Impact:
- Reskilling and Upskilling: Prepare the workforce for the changing job landscape.
- Social Safety Nets: Implement policies to support those affected by job displacement.

Ethical Guidelines and Regulations:
- Develop Ethical Guidelines: Establish clear ethical principles for AI development and deployment.
- Comply with Regulations: Adhere to relevant regulations and standards.

Real-World Implications of AI

- Healthcare: AI can improve medical diagnosis, drug discovery, and personalized treatment.
- Finance: AI can be used for fraud detection, risk assessment, and algorithmic trading.
- Transportation: Self-driving cars and autonomous vehicles can revolutionize transportation.
- Education: AI can personalize learning and improve educational outcomes.
- Climate Change: AI can help address climate change by optimizing energy consumption and developing sustainable solutions.

Challenges and Opportunities

- Bias and Discrimination: Addressing bias in AI requires careful data curation and model development.

- Job Displacement: The rise of AI may lead to job displacement, necessitating retraining and upskilling.
- Ethical Dilemmas: AI systems can make complex decisions with ethical implications.
- Regulatory Challenges: Developing appropriate regulations to govern AI is complex.

Promoting Responsible AI

- Collaboration: Foster collaboration between AI researchers, policymakers, and ethicists.
- Education and Awareness: Educate the public about AI and its potential impacts.
- Ethical Guidelines: Develop and enforce ethical guidelines for AI development and deployment.
- Transparent and Explainable AI: Make AI systems more transparent and understandable.
- Human Oversight: Ensure human oversight in critical decision-making processes.

By addressing these challenges and promoting responsible AI, you can harness the power of AI to benefit society while minimizing potential risks.

Chapter 12: The Future of AI and Serverless Computing

The future of AI and serverless computing is brimming with exciting possibilities. As technology continues to evolve, we can expect to see significant advancements in both fields.

The Future of AI

1. **Advanced AI Models:** We can anticipate the development of more sophisticated AI models capable of understanding and generating complex human language, images, and other forms of data.
2. **AI-Powered Automation:** AI will automate routine tasks, increasing efficiency and productivity.
3. **AI for Social Good:**AI can be used to address global challenges like climate change, healthcare, and education.
4. **Ethical AI:** There will be a growing focus on ethical AI, ensuring fairness, transparency, and accountability.
5. **AI and Human Collaboration:** AI will augment human capabilities, enabling us to work more effectively and creatively.

The Future of Serverless Computing

1. **Serverless-First Development:** Serverless computing will become the default approach for building applications.
2. **Edge Computing and Serverless:** Serverless functions will be deployed at the edge to reduce latency and improve performance.
3. **Serverless Machine Learning:** More advanced machine learning models will be deployed serverlessly, enabling real-time predictions and insights.
4. **Serverless for IoT:** Serverless functions will be used to process data from IoT devices in real-time.
5. **Serverless for Data Engineering:** Serverless platforms will be used to build and manage data pipelines.

The Intersection of AI and Serverless Computing

- AI-Powered Serverless Functions: Serverless functions can be used to deploy AI models and trigger them based on events.
- Serverless AI Development: Serverless platforms can accelerate AI development by providing a scalable and cost-effective environment.
- AI-Driven Automation: AI can be used to automate the deployment and management of serverless applications.

As AI and serverless computing continue to evolve, it is essential to consider the ethical implications and societal impact of these technologies. By developing and deploying AI responsibly, we can harness the power of these technologies to create a better future.

Emerging Trends and Technologies

The landscape of technology is constantly evolving, with new trends and innovations emerging rapidly. Here are some of the most promising trends that are shaping the future:

Artificial Intelligence and Machine Learning

- Generative AI: Models like GPT-4 are capable of generating human-quality text, code, and art.
- AI-Powered Automation: AI is automating tasks across industries, from customer service to software development.
- Ethical AI: There's a growing focus on developing AI systems that are fair, unbiased, and transparent.

Cloud Computing

- Edge Computing: Processing data closer to the source to reduce latency and improve performance.
- Serverless Computing: A cloud computing model where the cloud provider automatically manages the allocation of machine resources.
- Multi-Cloud and Hybrid Cloud: Organizations are adopting hybrid and multi-cloud strategies to leverage the best of different cloud providers.

Internet of Things (IoT)

- IoT Security: Addressing security vulnerabilities and protecting IoT devices from cyberattacks.
- IoT Analytics: Analyzing massive amounts of data generated by IoT devices to derive insights.
- AI-Powered IoT: Integrating AI into IoT devices to enable intelligent decision-making.

Blockchain Technology

- Decentralized Finance (DeFi): Building financial applications on blockchain technology.
- Supply Chain Transparency: Using blockchain to track the origin and movement of goods.
- NFT (Non-Fungible Token): Digital assets representing ownership of unique items.

Cybersecurity

- Zero-Trust Security: A security model that assumes no one or nothing can be trusted.
- AI-Powered Cybersecurity: Using AI to detect and respond to cyber threats.
- Quantum Computing and Cybersecurity: Preparing for the potential impact of quantum computing on cybersecurity.

Quantum Computing

- Quantum Machine Learning: Leveraging quantum computing to accelerate machine learning algorithms.
- Quantum Cryptography: Developing quantum-resistant cryptographic algorithms.
- Quantum Simulation: Simulating quantum systems to understand and develop new materials and drugs.

Metaverse

- Virtual and Augmented Reality: Immersive experiences that blend the physical and digital worlds.

- Social and Economic Impact: Exploring the potential of the metaverse for social interaction, commerce, and work.

By staying informed about these emerging trends, businesses and individuals can capitalize on new opportunities and adapt to the changing technological landscape.

AI and the Metaverse: A Synergistic Future

The convergence of AI and the metaverse is poised to revolutionize various industries and human experiences. As the metaverse evolves into a more immersive and interactive digital realm, AI will play a crucial role in shaping its development and functionality.

AI-Powered Metaverse Experiences

1. Personalized Experiences:
AI algorithms can analyze user data to tailor experiences, such as recommending content, customizing virtual environments, and adapting to individual preferences.

2. Realistic and Immersive Worlds:
- AI-driven graphics and physics engines can create highly realistic and immersive virtual worlds.
- AI can generate realistic characters and objects, making the metaverse more believable.

3. Natural Language Processing (NLP):
- NLP-powered AI can enable natural language interactions with virtual agents and other users.
- AI can translate languages in real-time, facilitating global communication within the metaverse.

4. Real-Time Translation:
- AI-powered translation tools can break down language barriers, enabling seamless communication between users from different cultural backgrounds.

5. Intelligent Agents and Avatars:

- AI-powered agents can assist users with tasks, provide information, and guide them through the metaverse.
- Users can create personalized avatars with AI-generated features, clothing, and accessories.

Ethical Considerations in the AI-Powered Metaverse

As AI becomes more integrated into the metaverse, it's crucial to address ethical concerns:

- Privacy: Protecting user data and privacy is paramount.
- Bias and Discrimination: Ensuring that AI algorithms are fair and unbiased.
- Digital Divide: Ensuring equitable access to the metaverse for all.
- Addiction and Mental Health: Monitoring and mitigating potential negative impacts on mental health.

The Future of AI and the Metaverse

The future of AI and the metaverse is bright. As technology continues to advance, we can expect to see even more innovative and immersive experiences. Some potential future developments include:

- AI-Generated Content: AI can generate realistic and creative content, such as music, art, and literature.
- AI-Powered Virtual Assistants: Intelligent virtual assistants can provide personalized assistance and support.
- AI-Driven Economic Opportunities: New economic opportunities will emerge as the metaverse grows.
- Ethical AI Frameworks: The development of robust ethical frameworks to guide the development and deployment of AI in the metaverse.

By addressing the challenges and embracing the opportunities, we can shape the future of AI and the metaverse in a way that benefits humanity.

The Role of AI in Sustainable Development

AI for Sustainable Development: A Powerful Tool

Artificial intelligence (AI) has the potential to revolutionize how we address global challenges and achieve sustainable development goals (SDGs). By harnessing the power of AI, we can optimize resource usage, reduce environmental impact, and improve social equity.

Key Areas Where AI Can Contribute to Sustainable Development

1. Climate Change Mitigation and Adaptation:
- Predictive Analytics: AI can predict climate patterns, natural disasters, and extreme weather events to aid in disaster preparedness and response.
- Energy Efficiency: AI-powered systems can optimize energy consumption in buildings, industries, and transportation.
- Renewable Energy: AI can optimize the performance of renewable energy sources, such as solar and wind power.

2. Sustainable Agriculture:
- Precision Agriculture: AI can analyze data from sensors and satellites to optimize crop yields and reduce the use of pesticides and fertilizers.
- Food Waste Reduction: AI-powered systems can predict demand and optimize supply chains to minimize food waste.

3. Sustainable Cities:
- Smart City Infrastructure: AI can optimize traffic flow, energy consumption, and waste management in urban areas.
- Sustainable Urban Planning: AI can help in urban planning, land use optimization, and infrastructure development.

4. Environmental Conservation:
- Wildlife Conservation: AI can monitor wildlife populations, detect illegal activities, and predict threats to biodiversity.

- Forest Conservation: AI can help track deforestation, monitor forest health, and optimize forest management practices.

5. Social Impact:
- Healthcare: AI can improve healthcare outcomes by accelerating drug discovery, personalized medicine, and disease diagnosis.
- Education: AI-powered personalized learning can enhance educational outcomes.
- Poverty Reduction: AI can help identify vulnerable populations and allocate resources effectively.

Challenges and Ethical Considerations

While AI offers immense potential for sustainable development, it's essential to address potential challenges and ethical concerns:

- Data Privacy: Ensuring the ethical collection and use of data.
- Algorithmic Bias: Mitigating bias in AI algorithms to avoid discriminatory outcomes.
- Job Displacement: Addressing the potential job displacement caused by automation.
- Environmental Impact: Minimizing the environmental impact of AI, particularly in terms of energy consumption and hardware production.

By carefully considering these challenges and implementing ethical guidelines, we can harness the power of AI to create a more sustainable future.

Appendix A: Additional Resources and Tools

Popular AI and ML Libraries

- TensorFlow: A popular open-source platform for building and deploying machine learning models.
- PyTorch: A flexible and efficient deep learning framework.
- Scikit-learn: A versatile machine learning library for classical machine learning algorithms.
- Keras: A high-level API built on top of TensorFlow and other frameworks.
- Hugging Face: A platform for sharing and using state-of-the-art machine learning models, especially for natural language processing.

Cloud Platform Documentation and Tutorials

- AWS Documentation: Comprehensive documentation for all AWS services, including tutorials, code samples, and best practices.
- Google Cloud Platform Documentation: Detailed documentation for GCP services, with tutorials and code labs.
- Microsoft Azure Documentation: Extensive documentation for Azure services, including tutorials, quickstarts, and how-to guides.

Online Courses and Certifications

- Coursera: Offers a wide range of machine learning and AI courses from top universities and institutions.
- edX: Provides online courses on machine learning, data science, and AI.
- Udacity: Offers nanodegrees and courses in machine learning and AI.
- Google Cloud Platform Certification: Certify your skills in Google Cloud Platform, including machine learning and data engineering.
- AWS Certification: Certify your skills in AWS, including machine learning and data analytics.
- Microsoft Azure Certification: Certify your skills in Azure, including machine learning and data science.

Additional Resources

- Kaggle: A platform for data science competitions and datasets.
- Papers With Code: A repository of machine learning papers and code implementations.
- OpenAI: A research laboratory focused on AI.
- Machine Learning Mastery: A blog and online course platform for machine learning.
- O'Reilly Media: A publisher of technical books and online learning resources.

By leveraging these resources, you can continue learning and growing your skills in AI and machine learning.

Appendix B: Case Studies

Case Study 1: AI in Healthcare

Problem: Accurate and early diagnosis of diseases.

Solution:

- Image Analysis: AI-powered image analysis tools can detect diseases like cancer from medical images (X-rays, CT scans, MRIs) with high accuracy.
- Drug Discovery: AI can accelerate drug discovery by analyzing vast amounts of biological data to identify potential drug candidates.
- Personalized Medicine: AI can analyze patient data to develop personalized treatment plans.

Case Study 2: AI in Finance

Problem: Fraud detection and risk assessment.

Solution:

- Fraud Detection: AI algorithms can analyze financial transactions to identify patterns indicative of fraud.
- Credit Scoring: AI-powered credit scoring models can assess creditworthiness more accurately.
- Algorithmic Trading: AI can analyze market data to make automated trading decisions.

Case Study 3: AI in Autonomous Vehicles

Problem: Developing self-driving cars.

Solution:

- Computer Vision: AI-powered computer vision systems enable cars to perceive their surroundings, including pedestrians, other vehicles, and traffic signs.
- Machine Learning: Machine learning algorithms can be used to train models to make decisions in real-time.
- Sensor Fusion: Combining data from various sensors (cameras, LiDAR, radar) to create a comprehensive understanding of the environment.

Case Study 4: AI in Customer Service

Problem: Improving customer service efficiency and satisfaction.

Solution:
- Chatbots: AI-powered chatbots can handle customer inquiries and provide support 24/7.
- Sentiment Analysis: AI can analyze customer feedback to identify sentiment and improve products and services.
- Personalized Recommendations: AI can recommend products and services based on customer preferences.

By leveraging AI, these industries can achieve significant improvements in efficiency, accuracy, and customer satisfaction.

Serverless Applications

Real-time Data Processing:

- IoT Data Processing: Serverless functions can process data from IoT devices in real-time, enabling applications like smart homes, smart cities, and industrial IoT.
- Log Analysis: Serverless functions can analyze logs to identify anomalies and security threats.

Web and Mobile Backends:

- API Backends: Serverless functions can be used to build APIs for web and mobile applications, scaling automatically to handle varying loads.
- Microservices Architectures: Serverless functions can be used to build microservices, enabling a modular and scalable architecture.

Image and Video Processing:

- Image and Video Analysis: Serverless functions can process images and videos for tasks like object detection, facial recognition, and content moderation.

Machine Learning Model Deployment:
- Model Serving: Serverless functions can be used to deploy machine learning models, making real-time predictions.
- Model Retraining: Serverless functions can be scheduled to retrain models periodically.

By combining AI and serverless computing, businesses can build innovative applications that are scalable, cost-effective, and responsive to changing demands.